Fun with

SSF

Secret Writing

Geoffrey Lamb

Bibliographical Note

This Dover edition, first published in 2002, is an unabridged republication,
with minor corrections, of the work published as *Secret Writing Tricks* by
Thomas Nelson Inc., Publishers, Nashville, Tennessee in 1975.

Library of Congress Cataloging-in-Publication Data

Lamb, Geoffrey Frederick.
   [Secret writing tricks]
   Fun with secret writing / Geoffrey Lamb.
      p. cm.
   Originally published: Secret writing tricks. Nashville, Tenn. : T. Nelson,
1975.
   Summary: Examines a number of different ways of writing secret messages, including using invisible ink and a variety of ciphers. Provides sug-
gestions and aids for code-breaking.
   ISBN 0-486-42098-1
   1. Cryptography—Juvenile literature. 2. Ciphers—Juvenile literature.
[1. Cryptography. 2. Ciphers.] I. Title.

Z103.3 .L35 2002
652'.8—dc21

                             2001054299

Manufactured in the United States of America
Dover Publications, Inc., 31 East 2nd Street, Mineola, N.Y. 11501

CONTENTS

TERMS USED IN THIS BOOK

Plain writing. Ordinary writing (i.e., not in cipher form). Also known as clear writing.

To encipher. To change plain writing into cipher form.

To decipher. To change secret (enciphered) writing into plain writing, with or without the key.

To transcribe. To turn secret writing into plain writing, using the known code or cipher. The term is borrowed from shorthand.

Code. Strictly speaking, in a code whole *words* are substituted for other words or phrases, often arbitrarily. In a cipher the individual *letters* of a message are either rearranged or replaced by different letters or other symbols. The term "code-breaking," however, is often used in place of "cipher-breaking."

To break a cipher. To work out the meaning of an enciphered message without possessing the key to it.

Code-breaker. A person who does this, also known as a cryptanalyst.

Cryptogram. A message in cipher or code.

Cryptography. The art or study of secret writing.

Cryptanalysis. The art of breaking ciphers.

Right person. One for whom the secret message is intended.

Wrong person. Anyone for whom the secret message is not intended and who tries to discover its meaning.

Null. Letter or numeral without meaning, included in a message in order to confuse the wrong person.

Letter frequency. The number of times a letter of the alphabet occurs (or is likely to occur) in an ordinary piece of writing.

MOVING AHEAD

Can you read the following words?

GVO XJUI TFDSFU XSJUJOH

If you are used to reading ciphers, it may not take you very long to understand this. The words are written in one of the simplest ciphers ever invented.

But perhaps you are not yet familiar with the art of secret writing. Perhaps these strange-looking words are as mysterious to you as if they were written in a queer foreign language.

Here is the clue to the cipher. Instead of writing the letter B, for example, we write C. Instead of writing C we write D. Instead of writing Y we write Z. In other words, for each letter of the alphabet we substitute the letter which immediately follows. (For Z we substitute A.)

To decipher the message, of course, we reverse the process. For C we read B; for D we read C; for Z we read Y; and so on throughout the alphabet.

Use this clue to read the words at the beginning of the chapter. You will find that they give you the title of a familiar book.

Such a cipher is easy to write, and almost equally easy to read if you know the clue. However, it is not very difficult for the wrong person to read the message, for this cipher is very well known.

It becomes rather more effective if we move, say, three letters ahead instead of only one. That is to say, if we write D for A, E for B, and so on.

This three-ahead substitution is often known as the Julius Caesar cipher. It was probably invented, in fact, long before Caesar's time, but because he employed this form of secret writing in his dispatches his name has become attached to it. Try writing the name of this book in the Julius Caesar cipher.

The three-ahead system is not quite so easy to write and read as the one-ahead. But you can use it without much difficulty if you write out the alphabet in capital letters on two strips of paper, as shown below.

ABCDEFGHIJKLMNOPQRSTUVWXYZ
ABCDEFGHIJKLMNOPQRSTUVWXYZABCDEFGHIJKLMNOPQRSTUVWXYZ

You will notice that the lower strip is much longer than the upper and has the alphabet repeated. This is so that the upper strip can be moved along either backward or forward above the lower. The purpose of this will be seen in the next chapter.

With the aid of these strips placed as in the example, we can see at a glance that when D (longer strip) stands for A, then E will stand for B, J for G, S for P, B for Y, and so on.

In making the strips it is important to keep exactly the same amount of space between each letter. If you find this difficult, try cutting lined paper into narrow strips; the strips should run from top to bottom of the page. The lines will provide you with exactly equal divisions. Since you will need twenty-six divisions for the shorter strip and fifty-two for the longer, you will probably have to stick two or more strips together to get the required length. Alternatively, squared or graph paper could be used.

One advantage of this cipher is that you do not have to remember any elaborate secret clues either to write it or to read it. You simply write out the alphabet on two strips of paper, and the substitution becomes automatic.

Now that you are familiar with the secret clue of the Julius Caesar system you should be able to read the following:

WKH DUW RI VHFUHW ZULWLQJ LV
VRPHWLPHV FDOOHG FUBSWRJUDSKB

Don't forget that when you are transcribing a cipher message into plain writing, you first find the letter in the longer strip. Then you note the letter directly above it in the shorter strip.

Here is an important message in the same cipher. What does it say?

DOZDBV ORRN ERWK ZDBV EHIRUH BRX FURVV
WKH URDG

USING A KEY LETTER

The last chapter dealt with the three-ahead system. But a four-ahead, or six-ahead, or ten-ahead system could be used equally easily by moving the shorter strip the right number of places along.

However, what about the reader of the message? If he doesn't know whether it is written in, say, four-ahead or twelve-ahead cipher, it will take him some time to discover what you are trying to tell him!

The easiest way of overcoming this difficulty is to stick always to the same system. If your cipher is always, say, five letters ahead, the reader will know just how to unravel the message.

The weakness of this is that if the wrong person, by experiment or accident, discovers that you always write in five-ahead cipher, your secrets will no longer be secret.

However, it is possible to defeat him by changing your system every time you send a message and by including in the message a clue which the wrong person will not understand. This clue is known as the *key letter*.

The key letter is the one which is substituted for A— in other words, the letter that comes directly under A when the shorter strip is moved. (In the three-ahead system the key letter is D.) Get this key letter in the right place and all the other letters will automatically fall into the right place too.

You can indicate the key letter by arranging with your friend that, for example, it will always be added to the end of the *third* word of the message. Then, as soon as he receives the message, he will note the last letter of the third word and will move the shorter strip until the letter A comes directly above this key letter.

The key letter is, of course, disregarded in reading the actual message.

Such a system is fairly safe for ordinary purposes, but it is still possible for the wrong person to discover the secret by painstaking effort. Extra difficulty can be added, however, by varying the key letter for *each word* of the message.

Care is needed in doing this, or both you and the reader will get into a muddle. The best plan is to choose a simple word and make this the clue to the changing key letters. For example, take the word "Brownie." Then the key letter for the first word in the message will be B. For the second word the key letter will be R; for the third word it will be O; for the fourth it will be W; and so on until E is reached.

There are seven letters in the word "Brownie." If your message consists of more than seven words, you will start at B again for the eighth word and work through the word "Brownie" for a second time (and, if necessary, for a third or fourth time, or as many times as required).

Let us take an example. Suppose our message is the simple statement: *This is the second chapter of your secret writing book.*

Our key word is "Brownie." As B is the first letter of the key word, we begin by placing the upper (shorter) strip so that the letter A comes directly above B in the lower strip. We are now ready to deal with the first word of the message. We look for T in the shorter strip. The letter which comes directly below it (as you will see if you try it out) is U, and so instead of writing T we write U. Similarly, instead of writing H, I, S, we write the letters which fall directly beneath these (i.e., I, J, T).

For the second word of the message we use R (the second letter of "Brownie") as our key letter, moving the letter A in the shorter strip until it comes directly above R. Instead of writing the word "is," we write the letters which now fall immediately below I and S—namely Z and J.

For the third word of the message the A of the shorter strip is moved until it is above O, the third letter of "Brownie," and the same process is continued until the message is complete.

Here is part of the message set out so as to show precisely how the ciphering is done. Finish it for yourself.

b	r	o	w	n	i	e	b
THIS	IS	THE	SECOND	CHAPTER	OF	YOUR	SECRET
UIJT	ZJ	HVS	OAYKJZ	PUNCGRE	WN	CSYV	TFDSFU

(Note that the letters of the key word are written above each word of the message, to avoid mistakes.)

This is a very difficult type of cipher for anyone not in the know to deal with. Most people would be quite unable to break it.

Here is a simple message for you to transcribe:

BT PFL YBCK SDWP GUR KTCM MW, OP UFLSK MCI SANA NOYR BW VIEH UIJT DVJJRXV KWHVCIH WJU GEBHOYR

Begin by copying out the ciphered message and then writing the letters b, r, o, w, n, i, e above each word.

The following is a very short story:

UXP DVE KSFS OEPPEJC VA I VEMPAEC DBSSJBHF. "ZMV BSJSF OAAJ N OPWAB," WEMH POF DRE. "MSG UKQ UNIR," AIQL XLI PUIFS—REU JOBWGVSR.

Instead of using the word "Brownie" (which will by now be known to all readers of this book), you can choose a word of your own as the key word. The secret will then belong only to yourself and the person to whom you may wish to pass a message.

FIVE-LETTER WORDS

Suppose you discovered the following cipher message:

YFVUV NOWVI KTOHL SKETC BRFEV TXWCR HIRTU IDNFG

You might decide that this was some form of Julius
Caesar cipher, and you could spend several hours trying
to work out which letters were substituted for which
other letters.

You would be wasting your time. The cipher above is
not a substitution one. It is a much simpler affair—one
that can be written very quickly and read without any
trouble at all. Yet unless you are in on the secret, you
may well find it far from easy to deal with.

Just try picking out every other letter of the message
(i.e., the second and each alternate letter). Jot these letters down, divide them into proper words, and once
more you will discover a familiar book title.

Simple though it is, this kind of cipher can be quite
puzzling, especially to someone who is looking for a
more elaborate system.

The cipher is simplicity itself to write. The first letter can be any that you please. The next is the first genuine letter of the message. Then, before every other
genuine letter, you put a letter chosen at random. Just
check, as you write, that the genuine letters are falling
alternately.

Such a cipher is very easy to transcribe when you
know what to look for. See how long it takes you to read
the following:

7

(i) HBRES WYADR KETOU FMASM DASNR WHELA
KRBIO NTGLA DYSEB LRLMO MWSTU IVEMD
(ii) SHOES INSTO LURTA TKOMK PIRLJ LDYHO SUPPH
(iii) ATRHO RLOVW XPMEN PQPRE MRLIF NDHSI DSTFR
ANCOE STROS MUALK LETHB ILMYS UNDER ERZKE

A disadvantage of this system is that every word
becomes twice as long as it would normally be. This
would be even more of a disadvantage if the words
were not split up into small groups of letters, for a
number of very long words would suggest to a code-
breaker which system was being used. By making each
cipher word consist of exactly five letters—a common
practice in cipher writing—we give him no such clue.

Here are two messages in five-letter cipher:

(i) LIQFD YTOKU RKLEJ EMPEA LDBIM AVRTY RAXBL
ORUWT VYKOC UTRBP URDIN VMAST LERLO IPFQE
STNRH YJUBS VIKNI GBALC WIXPD HAEDR
(ii) RTPHS IKSXW VIBLG LBERN HAPBC LFESY DORUK
TVOWK MEKEB PDYDO MULRD SVEDC QRAEW TXSDF
LRTOX MSPHR VYSIK NCGME WYKEO SBCDX

It is possible, of course, to use variations of the system. For example, can you read the following?

HYRKO EUFXR TBZCO EOLGK VOJTF KSRDE FCALR
PEQZT BWEOR ZIUHT JIXTN WGJBX

This is very easy indeed to write, and almost equally
easy to read if you know the secret. If you have not
already solved the puzzle, try picking out the second
and last letters of each word.

Such a system is obviously more suitable for fairly
short messages than for long ones.

SECRETS OF A BISHOP

The kind of cipher described in the last chapter was really invented (or at any rate first described) by a bishop. John Wilkins (1614–1672), Bishop of Chester, was the author of one of the first books in English devoted to secret writing. It was entitled *Mercury, or the Secret and Swift Messenger,* and was first published in 1647.

His description of the cipher states that "only the first, middle, and last letters are significant." The example he gives is:

Fildy fagodur wyndeeldrare discogverantibred

which means

FiLdY FagOduR WyndeEldrARE DISCOgVERantibrED.

You will see that in the first two words he kept precisely to the first, middle, and last letters, but subsequently used whole groups instead of single letters. This certainly keeps the message fairly short, but it also makes it easier for the wrong person to read it. For this reason, among others, the methods described in our last chapter are probably of greater practical value than the system of Bishop Wilkins.

Here is another cipher idea put forward by the bishop. According to this system, only the first five letters of the alphabet, arranged in pairs, are used to cover the whole alphabet.

A	B	C	D	E	F	G	H	I/J	K	L	M	N
aa	ab	ac	ad	ae	ba	bb	bc	bd	be	ca	cb	cc

O	P	Q	R	S	T	U	V	W	X	Y	Z
cd	ce	da	db	dc	dd	de	ea	eb	ec	ed	ee

e.g., *bd aacb abaedddbaaedaead* (I am betrayed).

This is ingenious, and the principle is easy to remember, but a very long word such as the third (sixteen letters) would suggest to a code-breaker that two letters were being used to represent a single ordinary letter. Hence he would guess that the letters were being used in pairs. Moreover, the fact that *aa* stands for A, *ab* for B, *ac* for C, *ad* for D, and *ae* for E could be something of a giveaway. With these hints to help him, an intelligent person might soon arrive at the secret.

There is no reason, however, why we should not adapt the bishop's scheme to form a more deceptive one. Instead of starting with *aa* = A, we could begin, for instance, with the letter D. We will also put the cipher letters in capitals, as these are easier to read.

d	e	f	g	h	i	j	k	l	m	n	o	p
AA	AB	AC	AD	AE	BA	BB	BC	BD	BE	CA	CB	CC

q	r	s	t	u	v	w	x	y	a	b	c
CD	CE	DA	DB	DC	DD	DE	EA	EB	EC	ED	EE

Note that the least common letter, Z, has been omitted. It can always be replaced by S.

If we now arrange the letters of a message in, say, three-letter or five-letter groups, the fact that they must be read in pairs will be quite well disguised, and there will be no very long words to arouse suspicion. The message *I am betrayed* might become:

BAE CBE EDA BDB CEE CEB ABA AEB

The last two letters of the message are nulls to make up a three-letter group.

To transcribe the message the reader simply marks off the letters in pairs:

BA / E C / BE / etc.

In writing a message you may find it easiest to begin by jotting down the whole message in pairs, afterward writing it out again with the letters in threes or fives.

The actual message can then be written out in three-letter or five-letter groups. Can you read the following plea?

DEA BEC CEA BBA CAA AAB DAC CAB CEE CDB ABC AAB
ABA ACB ACA EAB BDC CCD

Here is a notice in five-letter groups:

DBAEA BCEAB DEBAB DBDED ABECB EABAB DBBAC
AADCB ACCBD CCEDA ABEEC EABDB DACBE EBAAB
DBEBD BCBBE CBCEC ECBDE ECDBD BDECB BACAD
BAEAB EEABB DBDEC CECBA CDBAE ABCBB DAAAE
CBDCD AABCD

AROUND AND AROUND

This chapter deals with one of the oldest methods of secret writing. It was first used over two thousand years ago by the Spartans of ancient Greece, but you may still find it an entertaining way of sending a short secret message.

Let us first see how the message would look to anyone who discovered it. (See Figure 1.) It is written on a long strip of paper bearing an apparently meaningless jumble of letters. The strip is in fact too long to fit onto a single page of this book, and so for purposes of illustration it had to be broken in four.

I am sure you will agree that this strip cannot easily be understood as it stands. To bring out the sense, the decipherer must wind the strip around and around a cylinder of just the right size. Such a cylinder was known to the Romans as a *scytale* (pronounced "*sid*-del-lee").

Both the writer and the receiver of the message must have a cylinder of exactly the same size. The easiest thing to do is to take a round stick or rod and cut it in half, each person keeping one section. But there are various alternatives. For example, you might find a couple of toilet-paper-roll centers that are precisely the same size.

To use the cylinder, or scytale, fasten one end of a long thin strip of paper to it with a small piece of sticky transparent tape, or a drawing-pin. Then wind the strip tightly and evenly around the cylinder, and attach the other end as well, to keep it firm.

Write your message along the length of the wrapped scytale, taking care to put only one letter at a time on

H	R	P	F
J	S	R	H
E	D	T	K
T	M	S	T
A	G	M	A
A	M	Y	I
O	O	R	E
W	T	S	R
A	E	C	O
S	E	E	K
I	L	I	W
R	M	H	O
F	E	A	L
E	O	G	M
C	G	C	H
D	A	S	L
F	O	L	E
P	X	H	T
T	B	H	X
A	E	U	M
K	A	J	N
T	E	H	D
C	N	U	T
E	T	L	E
K	C	P	N
F	I	T	S
N	O	G	K
E	U	E	

Figure 1

each section of the strip. The letters must be kept level with each other as well as regularly spaced. It is best to use capitals.

Figure 2 shows what the message should look like. Of course, only a part of it is shown; the rest is on the other side of the scytale. Note that the message actually begins on the third section of the strip, not on the first. This helps to confuse the code-breaker. Two nulls, previously agreed upon (in this case the letters J, P), are

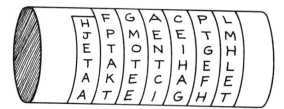

Figure 2

used as an indication to the reader that this is where the message starts.

When the message has been completed, any remaining spaces are filled up with other nulls. Figure 1 includes no fewer than twenty-eight nulls, and this would give the would-be code-breaker quite a headache!

The message partly revealed in Figure 2 is the one shown on the long strip in Figure 1. It reads in full: "Meet me tonight at the lake cafe at eight o'clock. We must make plans for hiding the treasure from Jones."

Although the quickest and easiest way of deciphering such a message is to find a cylinder of the correct size, it is sometimes possible to "break" the cipher without using a scytale. As the letters will normally be evenly spaced, an expert code-breaker may be able to discover, by trial and error, the right number of spaces between each letter of the message.

For this reason the scytale is of limited value as a cipher device unless its very existence is unknown to the enemy. In Roman times the letters were sometimes inscribed on the inside of a simple belt or sash, for instance, which would not, it was hoped, come under suspicion if the messenger was captured.

In spite of its limitations, the scytale can be great fun to use, and the amateur code-breaker would not find it at all easy to cope with such a message as that shown in Figure 1.

SECRECY IN NUMBERS

Cryptographers have always been attracted by numerical ciphers, with numbers standing for letters. Although such a system dates back to very early times, it became particularly popular during the seventeenth century. Many secret letters written by Charles I during England's Civil War begin in plain writing and then break off into a long sequence of numbers. Here is an example, sent to his chief commander during the siege of Oxford in 1642.

Besides what ye will receive in answer to your last dispatch by my Secretary I must add this *ni:* 5: 1: 57: 67: 64: 2: 81: 70: 44: 74: 82: 80: 45: 83: 15: *ni:* 11: 38: 3: 59: 79: 4: 66: 48: 69: 85: 25: 76: 58: 61: 75: 1: 78: 57: 86: 15: 59: 87: 67: 45: 75: 62: 58: 34: 16: 66: p5: 17:.

The letter continues with further numbers, and then concludes in plain writing: "This is all for the present I have tyme to wryte."

Writing of this kind is by no means easy to break. Unfortunately for the king, many of his letters were subsequently captured by his enemies. Some of the recipients had written the plain text above the numbers when they deciphered the messages, and valuable clues to the numerical cipher were thus obtained.

You may be wondering what Charles was saying in the message quoted above. Over the numbers are written these words: "to desire you to send to Chester as many musquets as you can spare," and the letter goes on to ask also for barrels of gunpowder. You will find that it is not altogether easy to match this plain text with the numbers. Letters of the alphabet appear to be represented by several different numbers, chosen apparently at random. (The symbol ni = to.)

A haphazard system of this kind has one great disadvantage. Both the writers and the readers must always keep a written copy of the system, showing exactly which numbers stand for which letters. If the copy is lost or mislaid, the writer or reader is in trouble, for a haphazard system cannot be reproduced from memory.

It is just as well, therefore, to devise a system which can be easily remembered. The simplest of all is to number the letters in alphabetical order, starting with A. Then 1 = A, 2 = B, and so on to 26 = Z. The word "cab" would thus be written: 3, 1, 2.

This system is very easy to write and read, but it is also rather obvious. We must be a little more subtle if we want to keep our secrets hidden.

A slight improvement would be to number the letters backward (e.g., 1 = Z, 2 = Y, etc.). Better, we could start our numbering in the middle (e.g., 1 = M, 2 = N, etc.). This can be reasonably puzzling to anyone who is not in the know. But what is really required is a system which seems to be haphazard but in fact is nothing of the kind.

Here is one way of achieving this. Arrange the numbers in three columns, numbering downward, with 1 to 8 in the first column, 9 to 17 in the second column, and 18 to 26 in the last. Then beginning, say, with M, write the letters of the alphabet *across* the columns, as in the table below.

1	M	9	N	18	O
2	P	10	Q	19	R
3	S	11	T	20	U
4	V	12	W	21	X
5	Y	13	A	22	B
6	C	14	D	23	E
7	F	15	G	24	H
8	I/J	16	K	25	L
		17	E	26	T

Note that there are two further subtleties here. As E and T are the two commonest letters of the alphabet, we have omitted Z (S can be used instead) and put I and J together,[1] so that E and T can have an extra number each.

If you put this table in alphabetical order (which is the easiest arrangement for *writing* a secret message), you get the following, which would be fairly confusing to the wrong person:

A	13	I/J	8	R	19
B	22	K	16	S	3
C	6	L	25	T	11, 26
D	14	M	1	U	20
E	17, 23	N	9	V	4
F	7	O	18	W	12
G	15	P	2	X	21
H	24	Q	10	Y	5

Here are three messages written in this numerical cipher. See how long it takes you to transcribe them. If you have a friend who also has a copy of this book, you can make a race of it. Remember that accuracy is

---

1. Up to the end of the seventeenth century I was commonly used for J.

important, so add, say, twenty seconds for every letter
incorrectly transcribed.

(i) 24, 17, 19, 23, 8, 3, 18, 9, 17, 12, 13, 5, 18, 7, 7,
     18, 19, 1, 8, 9, 15, 13, 3, 17, 6, 19, 23, 11, 2, 13,
     3, 3, 12, 18, 19, 14, 12, 24, 8, 6, 24, 6, 13, 9, 11,
     17, 13, 3, 8, 25, 5, 22, 23, 14, 8, 3, 6, 18, 4, 23, 19,
     17, 14.

(ii) 26, 13, 16, 17, 1, 18, 3, 11, 18, 7, 11, 24, 23, 25,
      17, 26, 11, 23, 19, 3, 8, 9, 5, 18, 20, 19, 18, 12, 9,
      9, 13, 1, 17, 13, 9, 14, 13, 19, 19, 13, 9, 15, 17, 11,
      24, 23, 1, 26, 18, 7, 18, 19, 1, 14, 8, 7, 7, 17, 19,
      23, 9, 11, 12, 18, 19, 14, 3.

(iii) 7, 18, 19, 17, 21, 13, 1, 2, 25, 23, 8, 13, 6, 16, 3,
       1, 8, 11, 24, 6, 18, 20, 25, 14, 22, 17, 1, 13, 14, 23,
       8, 9, 26, 18, "11, 24, 8, 6, 16, 8, 13, 1," 13, 9, 14,
       1, 13, 19, 5, 22, 19, 18, 12, 9, 8, 9, 11, 18, "12, 13,
       19, 1, 22, 18, 5."

(Don't forget that 8 can be either I or J; you
must use your intelligence to decide which.)

There are many variations of this system which
could be devised if you want to have a secret numerical
cipher of your own. For example, you could start the
numbering with a different letter (instead of M), or you
could have a different arrangement of columns.

Another very useful variation is to start your numbering with a double figure (e.g., 21), leaving out all single figures. Then it will not be necessary to use commas
to separate the numbers, as the right reader will know
that all the numbers have to be split up into pairs. If
you like, you can divide the figures into groups which
look like words (some with even numbers of figures,
some with odd ones), which will confuse the wrong
reader even further.

Here is a message written in this fashion. The numbering is very simple with A = 21, B = 22, and so on. But note that I and J have separate numbers.

29264535 41232134 432 13231 353 4402825
23252932 293427 432940283 54140 26213 23229
3427352 62645354138 2521332127292 3292134

Begin by dividing the figures into pairs, ignoring the spaces between words.

DOTS AND PINPRICKS

One of the subtlest methods of secret communication does not involve any actual writing at all. The ciphering is all done with the point of a pencil or pin.

The system may well have developed from a practice which had nothing to do with ciphers or cryptograms. There was a time, about 150 years ago, when to send a letter cost an Englishman a shilling (equivalent to about a dollar in present-day American values). On the other hand, a newspaper could be sent by post for nothing, for in those days newspapers had to pay a government tax and therefore bore a government stamp.

People who resented or could not afford the high cost of letter writing sometimes adopted an ingenious method of sending messages to their friends. They would mark an old newspaper in such a way that it conveyed personal news, and then send it by post without payment.

A letter written on the margins of the newspaper would have been easily detected by the postal authorities. The method used was therefore more subtle, though quite simple. In a particular column on a certain page, agreed upon beforehand, various letters would be picked out by having a pencil dot or pinprick placed beneath them. When the friend received the newspaper, he would write down these letters in the order in which they occurred. In due course he would find himself with a nice newsy letter.

Here is a newspaper item with certain letters bearing a dot beneath them. Write down these letters in order.

You will find that they give you a piece of information. What is it?

ḤAMBLE'S GREAT WELCOME
FOR CHAY ḄLYTH

Chay Blyth's ḷoud and tumultuous wẹlcome at Port Hamble took the small yachtịng village by ṣtorm as aṇ estimatẹd crowd of 8,000 surged onto the wạterfront.

The ex-paṛatrooper from Ṣcotland looked remarkably fit after spending ten mọnths sailing nonstop alone roụnd ṭhe world "tḥe wrong wạy round" (froṃ east to west).

The yacht's ṗale blue hull gleamed in the sunshine, showing no sigṇ of ṭhe battering she had received thrọugh some of the stormiest seas iṇ the world.

(August 1971)

Here is another short news paragraph, written while Blyth was still making his famous journey:

ÇHAY BLYTH SAỊLS
ROUND THE WOṚLD

Çhay Blyth last night sent oụt a radio ṃessage to Londoṇ that he hạs completed the first solo nonstop ỵoyage around the world from east to west—most of the way agaịnst all the prevailing winds and currents. He sạid that on Monday he crossed the ouṭward track of hịs voyage 300 miles frọm the Cape Verde Islaṇds.

(June 1971)

If you note down the dotted letters in the above passage, you will find that they give you a word meaning "voyage around the world."

There is, of course, nothing very secret about this piece of information! These two brief news items are given simply to show you how the dot ciphering is done.

Write out the first passage (omitting the headline) and then secretly indicate by dots the following urgent message: "You are in great danger. Beware of Ted."

Now can you write out the second news item and mark it with dots to convey a warning of some kind? Give it to a friend to decipher.

So far we have been dealing with the dot method of ciphering in its easiest form. But if we wanted to pass on a really secret message to a friend, it would be unwise to do so in exactly this way. It is just possible that someone else might notice the dots. He or she might have little difficulty in reading the message. We must therefore be a little more subtle in our method.

One thing we could do, of course, would be to put the message in a moving-ahead cipher, for example, such as the Julius Caesar system, before making the dots. Our friend would naturally have to know this cipher as well as being prepared to look out for the dots.

Here is another effective way of disguising the dots.

CHAY BLYTH SAILS
ROUND THE WORLD

Chay Blyth last night sent out a radio message to London that he has completed the first solo nonstop voyage around the world from east to west—most of the way against all the prevailing winds and currents. He said that on Monday he crossed the outward track of his voyage 300 miles from the Cape Verde Islands.

(June 1971)

Pick out the dotted letters and you will find that they spell the message: HGAONOSLALWNSDND. Can you interpret this?

These mysterious letters, in fact, represent once again the word meaning "voyage around the world."

The clue lies in the placing of the dots. Each dot is placed immediately *after* the letter to be read. Thus the first dot is placed under the H of "Chay" instead of under the C, and so on throughout the paragraph.

The two short news items given in this chapter have

been chosen deliberately to save space. But if you were using an actual newspaper, you could allow the dots to be spread over a whole column or more. Spaced at long intervals, they would hardly be noticed by anyone except the person looking for them.

Imagine you are a secret service agent wishing to communicate with a colleague by means of the dot-under-the-following-letter cipher. Take any newspaper and encipher a suitable message.

∇⊐L ∇⊐∪⊏∇⌐∪⊏∇⊓L ∪⊐⌐⊐L⌐

THE TICKTACKTOE CIPHER

You may think that the above is some ancient Egyptian inscription. However, it is merely another form of secret writing, and quite a common one.

This type of cryptogram is sometimes known as the Rosicrucian cipher, because a form of it was supposed to have been used by a secret society known as the Rosicrucians, founded in the seventeenth century.

During the Civil War the same kind of writing was freely used by soldiers of the northern states, who referred to it as the Pigpen cipher. You will see why if you look at the basic diagram. (See Figure 1.) This vaguely suggests the kind of pens in which farmers kept their pigs.

However, it also resembles the diagram used for playing Ticktacktoe, which most of us are more familiar with than with Rosicrucians or pigpens. So perhaps the best name for the system is the Ticktacktoe cipher.

There are several ways in which the system can be used. Figure 2 shows one of the simplest.

You will see that the letters are arranged in pairs. If we want to represent the *first* letter of a pair, then we

Figure 1   Figure 2

draw that part of the diagram in which the letter stands. If we want to represent the *second* letter of a pair, we draw the same part of the diagram but with a dot added. These examples will illustrate this:

$$A = \lrcorner \quad C = \sqcup \quad Q = \ulcorner \quad S = \lor$$
$$B = \dot{\lrcorner} \quad D = \dot{\sqcup} \quad R = \dot{\ulcorner} \quad T = \dot{\lor}$$

You are now in a position to work out the meaning of the secret writing at the beginning of this chapter.

The Ticktacktoe cipher is an ingenious system. One of its weaknesses, however, is that it has been used so many times that it has become known to quite a lot of people. If the letters are arranged in the regular order shown above, it is not too difficult for a code-breaker to find out the system that is being used.

We can make things much more difficult for him by arranging the letters in a more irregular order. But unless we can easily remember this order, we shall find ourselves in trouble if we mislay our copy of the diagram.

Is there any way in which an irregular order can conveniently be remembered? Yes, there is. Look at Figure 3.

You will see that eighteen letters of the alphabet have been set out in a mixed order, but this order is easily remembered because the letters form the three simple words: "adjust," "benzol," and "chirpy." Eight letters are left over, and these are fitted, in alphabetical order, into the big cross, moving in a clockwise direction from the top. An easy way of remembering the order of these letters (to save working it out) is to think of the words: FiG, KiM, QuiVer, WaX.

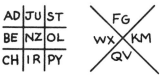

Figure 3

Whenever you want to send a message by this cipher, or to make a secret diary entry, you can quickly scribble the diagrams on a slip of paper, which can afterward be destroyed so that it does not fall into the hands of the wrong person.

What does this mean?

Here are two messages from a member of a secret organization. Can you read them?

(i) ⊐ ⌐⌐ ⌐⌐ ⌐⌐

(ii) ⌐⌐ ⌐⌐

Can you put the following into Ticktacktoe cipher? They are sentences taken from a secret letter, partly written in Pigpen, sent by a Northern agent during the Civil War.

   (i) Over a thousand muskets came duly to hand and were shipped to Halifax as instructed.

   (ii) We will be able to seize the other two steamers as per program.

If you want to make your own version of the Ticktacktoe cipher, you can arrange the three words ("adjust," "benzol," "chirpy") in a different way, or you can use three other words. But remember that whatever words you choose must cover eighteen letters all different from each other, and that the other eight letters must be arranged in the cross.

OPEN SPACES

One of the famous Sherlock Holmes stories by Sir Arthur Conan Doyle starts with a curious message received by a wealthy landowner.

> The supply of game for London is going steadily up. Head keeper Hudson, we believe, has now been told to receive all orders for flypaper, and for preservation of your hen pheasant's life.

Naturally the great detective, after a little experimenting, succeeded in deciphering this seemingly nonsensical note. The solution lay in taking the first and then every third word and ignoring the rest. Work this out for yourself (a hyphenated word counts as two) and you will see that the message is anything but nonsensical.

To discover why it came to be written, you must read the story. (It is called "The Gloria Scott" and is to be found in *The Memoirs of Sherlock Holmes*.) But *how* it was written is a matter that closely concerns us in this chapter.

The important words are written first, with spaces between them. These spaces are then filled in with any words that seem to make some sort of sense but are entirely unconnected with the real message. The writer of the note in the Sherlock Holmes story was in rather a hurry. If he had had more time, he might have been able to write a more sensible-seeming note. See if you can write one bearing exactly the same real message, with the same number of spaces between the important words.

It would have been harder for the detective to

decipher the message if the significant words had not occurred at regular intervals. One way of achieving this irregularity (without bewildering the right reader of the message) is to use what is known as a grid or grill. This is a card with holes spaced at varying intervals. This is placed over a piece of paper the same size as the grill, and the words of the secret message are written in the open spaces. The grill is then removed and the gaps between the words are filled in with any suitable words and phrases.

The right reader of the message has an exactly similar grill which he places over the paper. It is then easy for him to read the secret communication.

The device is sometimes known as a Cardan grill, as it was invented by a clever Italian mathematician named Geronimo Cardano, who lived in the seventeenth century.

It can, however, be quite hard to fill in the gaps with words that are exactly the right length and which also make natural sense. A more practical form of the Cardan grill, therefore, is one which uses letters instead of words. This grill is usually square in shape. Holes are cut at irregular intervals in the card, each hole being large enough for one letter to be written. (See Figure 1.)

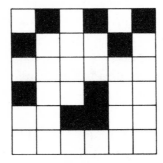

Figure 1

The square grill is placed on a piece of paper of the same size, and the first letters of the message are written through the holes. The grill is then given a quarter turn counterclockwise—which means that what was formerly the top of the grill is now on the left-hand side. Again the grill is placed on the paper, which has *not* been turned. As the holes no longer coincide with the letters that have already been written, the message can be continued.

When the nine holes have again been used up, the grill is given another quarter-turn, and the message is continued once more.

If the message is fairly short, any spaces left unfilled must be supplied with nulls. If it is fairly long, then a second square of paper will be required.

For the grill to be effective it must obviously be so designed that even if it is given *three* quarter-turns, no hole occurs at a place which already bears a letter. You may well find that it is by no means easy to invent a pattern of your own which has this merit. In this case you can copy the design shown in Figure 1.

Draw a line on a piece of stiff card (e.g., a postcard) and mark it off into six equal parts. At the beginning of this line draw another line at right angles, and mark this off in exactly the same way. This gives you the basis for a large square divided into thirty-six equal (smaller) squares, as in Figure 1. Mark the nine small squares that are black in the diagram; then cut out these squares on the card, using a sharp knife. You will now have a useful Cardan grill. (If you can manage to leave a border around your grill, this will help to keep it firm.)

Here is an example of a Cardan grill message. Can you read it? Begin by writing these letters on a square of paper exactly the same size as your grill.

N	Y	R	O	E	U
W	D	E	R	I	E
G	L	T	O	L	H
L	L	E	L	D	W
U	E	F	I	O	O
A	N	K	D	T	D

It is possible to manage without a cut-out grill. Copy the letters onto a piece of *semitransparent* paper the same size as the diagram in Figure 1. Place this paper over the diagram and read off the letters which show against the black squares. Turn the book around as many times as you find necessary to complete the message. Be prepared for a few nulls at the end.

Now write a message of your own, using a grill, and give it to a friend to read. Let him first try to decipher it as it stands. If he cannot, let him use the grill.

THE CROSSWORD GRILL

If you don't wish to cut a Cardan grill, or to make do with semitransparent paper, you can use what is sometimes known as a nonperforated grill. It rather resembles the regular and even pattern of a normal crossword puzzle, and a good name for it is the Crossword grill.

Because the pattern is regular it can easily be remembered, and so we do not need to keep a copy of it. As soon as we have used it for writing (or reading) a message, we can destroy the paper, and no one can steal or copy the grill. Secrecy is preserved.

The secret of using the Crossword grill is that the message is first written in the *white* squares, just like a crossword puzzle, and then written out again in four-letter (or five-letter) words as in an ordinary cipher message.

Begin by drawing a crossword outline. There is no fixed size, but nine columns across and nine down is quite a good number. Fill in some black squares to make a suitable design. Then write your message along the horizontal columns.

If you look at Figure 1 you will find that the message is: "Don't leave the building until you receive a signal from Frank." A few nulls have been added.

31

Figure 1

We now write out this message in four-letter words going *down* the columns. The result is:

ENYE MDEG OIGQ ABUV NFOV UUAR XNIN ELJT ELRF
AVTD TARN LIIE SOKH LCIK

The wrong reader would find it very hard indeed to "break" this, for the letters of the message do not occur at regular intervals. Even if he somehow discovered that the first letter of the message was D, he would be little further forward. The second letter, O, is thirteen spaces from the D, but the third letter, N, is only seven spaces from the O. This kind of thing makes the code-breaker tear his hair in despair.

The right reader, however, would have little difficulty in deciphering the message. He would first draw a nine-column square and fill in the black squares to produce the agreed design. Then he would write down the cipher message, putting the letters in the vertical columns, working down each column in turn. Having completed this task, he would simply read the message across the horizontal columns.

Now use the design in Figure 1 to read the following secret messages:

(i) OHRA ATHY ESCT SEAP HLHT CAHL SEHR YIQG IULM CVNR DCAO HCIL ATJT SYTS

(ii) HHIE NSAE TSHM EWOK EGEN EIMD EARL FINR DONS OTDF DOSC CTWG RISR RDTU

Make up a message of your own, using the same crossword pattern. Then write it out in four-letter words and give it to a friend to decipher. When he fails (as he almost certainly will), let him try again, this time using the crossword grill.

For complete secrecy you will need to make up your own crossword pattern. Be careful not to make it too complicated or you will find it hard to remember the design. Note that it is best to avoid having exactly the same number of black squares in each vertical column.

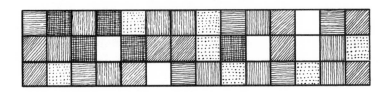

PRETTY PATTERNS

A fascinating and unusual cipher is one which employs no written symbols at all—no letters, no figures, no Ticktacktoe signs. Indeed, if you were not in on the secret, you might well think that what you are looking at is not a message at all but merely a pretty pattern, like the one at the head of this chapter.

You may perhaps be surprised to learn that this particular pattern, in fact, spells out (once again) the title of this book. (There is one null at the end.)

The pattern here is really less colorful than it would be if you drew it yourself. Each little square should be a certain color. In order to represent colors in a book printed in black and white, we have had to use symbols made up of lines and dots. (See Figure 1.) Anyone with

Black Green Blue Red Brown White

Figure 1

a few colored crayons, however, could write his secret message using nothing but colored squares.

Six colors are used, counting White as a color. The others, in alphabetical order, are Black, Blue, Brown, Green, and Red.

Each letter of the alphabet is represented by a *pair* of colors. Here is a table showing the system:

A = Black, Blue	J = Blue, White	R = Green, Brown
B = Black, Brown		S = Green, Red
C = Black, Green	K = Brown, Black	T = Green, White
D = Black, Red	L = Brown, Blue	
E = Black, White	M = Brown, Green	U = Red, Black
	N = Brown, Red	V = Red, Blue
F = Blue, Black	O = Brown, White	W = Red, Brown
G = Blue, Brown		X = Red, Green
H = Blue, Green	P = Green, Black	Y = Red, White
I = Blue, Red	Q = Green, Blue	

You will see that these colors are arranged throughout in alphabetical order, so that it is quite easy to write out this table from memory if you do not have the printed book handy.

It is best to use squared paper for the pattern which forms the message, but if you do not have any, you can easily draw your own squares.

It is quicker, though less impressive, to put dots instead of squares, but they need to be made bold and clear. A white dot would probably not be seen, so a tiny penciled circle can be drawn.

Yet another possibility is to write what looks like a message in, say, Julius Caesar cipher, using colored crayons for the letters. The right reader will entirely disregard the letters themselves; he will pay attention only to the colors, dividing them into pairs as with the colored squares. If you adopt this device, you will have to substitute Yellow, say, for White.

Can you decipher this pattern?

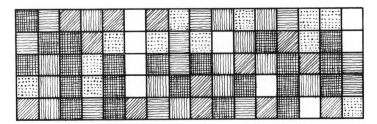

When you are deciphering a color cipher, perhaps the easiest and quickest way is to jot down the paired colors in note form before looking at the table to see which letters they represent. Thus you would begin to decipher the pattern at the head of this chapter by noting down: Bl, Bk / R, Bk / Br, R / R, Br /, and so on.

Just one other point. Extra symbols for the commonest letters (E, T, O, A, N, I, R, S, H) can be obtained if desired by using additional colors as the first of a pair. Thus an extra symbol for A could be Orange, Black; for E, Orange, Blue; for H, Orange, Brown; for I, Orange, Green; and so on, taking both letters and colors in alphabetical order.

THE REVOLVING CIRCLE

One of the most remarkable men of the seventeenth century was the Marquis of Worcester. Not only was he the inventor of the steam engine (in a primitive form), he also invented a portable bridge, a canal lock, and a paddle ship worked by a windmill on deck. Further, he had ideas for a flying machine, and he was one of the first men to plan an international language.

It is not surprising that so inventive a mind as his should be responsible for a neat secret writing device. In his book *The Century of Inventions* (1663) he described what is often known as a cipher wheel. This proved to be so useful that it has persisted through the centuries, at least in principle.

The cipher wheel is rather like the alphabet strips described in the first chapter of this book, but arranged in circular form instead of in straight lines. The wheel is a little harder to make than a couple of long strips, but it is great fun to use. The effort of making one is well worthwhile. It does need to be very accurately constructed, however, so if you are not very good at making this sort of thing, get a clever friend to make it for you.

Two circles are required, one slightly smaller than the other. Each circle bears a ring of letters. (See Figure 1.) The

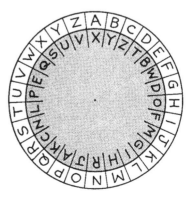

Figure 1

larger circle remains stationary. The smaller can be moved around and around.

If you examine Figure 1, you will see that the letters around the revolving (shaded) circle are spaced so that each letter is exactly opposite a letter in the larger circle. When the smaller circle is revolved, a different set of letters will be opposite those in the larger circle.

As there are twenty-six letters in the alphabet, there must be twenty-six spaces for them. These spaces must be exactly the same size and must be drawn so that those in the smaller circle match those in the larger. You may find that the easiest way to achieve this is to *trace* the circles and spaces in Figure 1, using paper that is fairly transparent. Afterward you can carefully cut out the smaller circle and paste it to a circular piece of card, thus making a cipher wheel that will stand a reasonable amount of handling. The card to which you paste the larger circle need not be circular.

Preferably use a geometry compass for tracing the circles, and a ruler for tracing the lines that divide the spaces. Use a paper clip to ensure that the paper does not move while you are tracing.

Having drawn your circles and spaces, you must next put in the letters. The outer circle has the letters in alphabetical order, starting with A near the top and working around in either a clockwise or an anticlockwise direction. The letters on the smaller circle could also be in alphabetical order, but it is better to jumble them up. This will make it much more difficult for your messages to be broken.

It is a good idea to use a key word or key phrase containing a number of different letters. For example, let us take the phrase TWO MIRACLES, which contains eleven different letters. Begin by arranging the phrase with each letter in *alternate* spaces. (See Figure 2.)

The remaining letters, in alphabetical order, are: B, D, F, G, H, J, K, N, P, Q, U, V, X, Y, Z. Fit these into the empty spaces as shown in the shaded circle in Figure 1. This gives a well-jumbled arrangement of letters, but one that can be easily remembered and repeated if the cipher wheel is mislaid. No

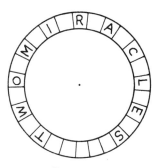

Figure 2

one else, however, could reproduce the arrangement unless he knew the key phrase.

Find a piece of thin wood or thick cardboard on which to place the circles. Now put the smaller circle within the larger, precisely in the center. Press a drawing pin through the exact center, and fasten the larger circle to the board with a piece of transparent adhesive tape. The smaller circle (or cipher wheel) can now be revolved at will.

To write a message in cipher is quite an easy task. But before you read any farther, you had better construct the two circles, or you will find it difficult to understand the following instructions.

Let us take as an example the simple message:

HIDE THE BOX UNDER THE HOLLY BUSH.

First we have to decide which letter of the revolving circle to place opposite to A in the fixed circle. An easy letter to remember is X (as in Figure 1).

To encipher the first word, "hide," find H in the fixed (larger) circle. The letter opposite this in the revolving circle is O. Next we find the letter opposite to I— namely, F. The letters opposite to D and E (in the larger circle) are respectively T and B (in the revolving circle). The first word of the cipher message is therefore OFTB.

It would be possible to keep the two circles in the same position for the whole of the message. But we can make things more difficult for the would-be code-breaker if we move the small circle each time we start a new word. For the second word of the message ("the"), we therefore turn the revolving circle one space back, bringing Y opposite to A. Then the word "the" will read PFW in cipher, as you will see if you try it out.

For the third word ("box") we revolve the circle another space back, bringing Z opposite to A. You will find that the enciphered word is TKV. Continuing to turn the revolving circle one space back for each new word, we finally encipher the whole message as follows:

OFTB PFW TKV SKDOP SIF HLKKT OXUR.

Note that the word "the" is enciphered in two entirely different ways (PFW and SIF) in this short message. This kind of change makes things very hard for the code-breaker.

To transcribe this message with the aid of the cipher wheel is by no means difficult. You simply reverse the process of enciphering the message.

Before beginning to read a message you may find it helpful, by using the cipher wheel, to work out which letter in the wheel will come opposite A for each word of the message. Thus it will be X for the first word, Y for the second, Z for the third, T for the fourth, and so on. Write these letters in brackets above the appropriate words of the message, as shown below. This will help you to check, as you go along, that you have the wheel in the right position for each word.

(X) (Y) (Z) (T) (B) (W) (D)
OFTB PFW TKV SKDOP SIF HLKKT OXUR

When X in the cipher wheel is opposite A in the fixed

circle, then O (first letter of the enciphered message) faces H in the fixed circle, and F faces I. Similarly, T faces D, and B faces E. Thus the first word is seen to be "hide."

Turn the cipher wheel one space back and continue with the next word, and so on with each succeeding word.

See if you can decipher the following three messages. Start each message with X (in the cipher wheel) opposite to A.

(i) TFT MP EZHD YCS ANCG UL SGDM XJAV PHXXFJH?

(ii) UJP RELP JKSD QGO EFVNAVHCG ORQOKM VZP VQOMIV MFGN MJZRX JGHC OVZJ PV XCGD XNDDJPN.

(iii) RJQ XKQ BEF OGFPNJLH HWSHVY GT DBPVN OEN NUWSPO JVQQT!

IMPORTANT

When *writing* a message, look for the letter in the fixed circle and *write* the letter appearing in the revolving circle.

When *deciphering* a message, look for the letter in the revolving circle and *write* the letter appearing in the fixed circle.

SECRET INKS

Invisible inks are sometimes used by secret agents. The main aim here is to disguise the fact that there has been any secret communication at all. Thus the message may be written along the margin of a newspaper, or on the inside of an envelope flap, or even underneath the stamp.

There are many liquids which can be used as secret inks, but a long list of chemicals would be out of place in a book of this kind. Here are just a few useful inks.

A pinch of ferrous sulfate dissolved in about a tablespoonful of water will produce brown writing when the paper is soaked in a solution of sodium carbonate (washing soda) and then dried. A heaping teaspoonful of soda to a glass of water will produce enough developer for most messages.

Simpler substances have been used. An aspirin tablet, which any agent can carry around without arousing suspicion, even if he is searched, will make an effective secret ink if dissolved in alcohol. To develop the message, the receiver merely dips a piece of absorbent cotton in alcohol and draws it across the paper where he knows the writing will be found.

But the simplest inks of all, and those which readers of this book will probably find it most convenient to use, are two liquids that can be found in almost every home—milk and lemon juice. Allowed to dry, both of these become reasonably unnoticeable unless used too thickly. To develop the writing, the receiver merely holds the paper close to an electric light bulb, or a few inches from an electric fire (taking great care not to let it catch fire), or presses it with a hot iron. The writing should appear in brown. You may find that lemon juice is the more effective of the two.

An ordinary nib is probably the best form of writing implement. It must obviously be quite clean or the writing will be far from invisible! If you have no nib available, sharpen the end of a matchstick to a point and use that.

CODE-BREAKING

Almost every country possesses an intelligence service, much of whose time is spent in trying to break the codes and ciphers of other nations. Sometimes enormous numbers of men and women are engaged in work connected with this kind of activity. The United States National Security Agency, for instance, employs about fifteen thousand people.

But code-breaking can also be performed by anyone interested in secret writing, simply for the fun of trying to solve a puzzle. Moreover, it is well worthwhile learning to break ciphers as a help toward improving your skill in writing them. To take a very simple instance: experience as a code-breaker will make it clear that a three-letter word that occurs several times in a message is likely to be either "the" or "and." When you are writing your own secret messages, therefore, you will be careful to avoid using these words or, alternatively, to disguise them in some way.

The first thing a code-breaker has to do is to decide whether the message before him is a Transposition cipher (such as the Cardan grill), or a Substitution cipher (such as the Julius Caesar).

Where the actual letters of the message are used but are arranged in unusual positions (as on page 9 or 32), we have a Transposition cipher. On the other hand, a message in figures or strange symbols must be some kind of Substitution cipher (i.e., something else is substituted for letters). A message in ordinary letters of the alphabet may also be a Substitution cipher if other letters are substituted for the real letters of the message.

If the cipher uses letters, begin by counting the number of times each individual letter is used in the message. The result may be something like this (with the figure in parentheses showing how many times each letter has been used): Z (12), K (10), V (8), B (8), L (7), Q (6), and so on down to T (1), O (1).

We now apply the rules of something known as Letter Frequency—one of the code-breaker's chief weapons. Some letters of the alphabet are used far more than others in written English. Careful surveys have shown that the nine most frequently used letters are E, T (the two commonest), O, N, A, I, R, S, H. (Think of the words "Etona" and "Irish" and you will find it easy to remember the nine letters.) The least commonly used letters are Z, Q, J, X, with K and V as runners-up.

The letter-count referred to in the paragraph above shows Z, K, and V as the letters most used, and T and O among those least used. This contradicts the rules of Letter Frequency, and so it is almost certain that we have a Substitution cipher. Probably Z has been substituted for E, and K substituted for T.

If, on the other hand, our counting had given us some such result as: E (11), T (10), O (8), R (8), down to K (2), J (1), we could be fairly certain that we were dealing with a Transposition cipher.

In dealing with a Substitution cipher, we need plenty of space above each line of the message. If the original does not have this space, we must supply it, copying the message very carefully and accurately with good spaces between the lines. Then, *in pencil*, we apply our Letter Frequency discoveries, writing E above the letter or symbol which occurs most often and T above the next on the list.

It will be best to take an actual example. Let us suppose that this is our cipher message:

RGVGT KU VJG ENGXGTGUV DQA KP VJG ENCUU CV
VTAKPI VQ UQNXG EKRJGTU

Letter counting gives the following results: G (9), V (7), U (6), K (4), T (4), J (3), E (3), Q (3). With all nine of the top Letter Frequency letters occurring less often than G, V, and U, it seems likely that this is a Substitution cipher, possibly with G standing for E, and V standing for T.

Let us, then, assume that G = e, V = t. Above each line of the message we write our assumed solution as far as it goes, adding dashes or dots where we think it might be useful.

```
- e t e -    t - e - - e - e - t        t - e       - t
RGVGT KU VJG ENGXGTGUV DQA KP VJG ENCUU CV
t - - - - - t -  - - - - e  - - - - e - -
VTAKPI VQ UQNXG EKRJGTU
```

A quick survey will suggest at once that our guesses are probably correct. The commonest three-letter word in English is "the." In this message we have one three-letter word (VJG) used twice, and our experiment gives us *t-e* for this word. It is therefore highly probable that we were correct in assuming that V = t and G = e, and it is also likely that J = h.

Another point also strikes us. There are four two-letter words, and if V = t, then one of these words is -*t*, and another is *t*-. There is only one ordinary two-letter word in English beginning with *t*—namely, "to." If VQ = *to*, then Q = *o*.

We therefore add *h* and *o* to our experimental substitution, which gives us:

```
- e t e -    t h e - - e - e - e - t  - o -    t h e        - t
RGVGT KU VJG ENGXGTGUV DQA KP VJG ENCUU CV
t - - - - - t o - o - - e - - - h e - -
VTAKPI VQ UQNXG EKRJGTU
```

We still have to find which letter is represented by U (6), and we still have A, N, I, R, and S among our commonly used letters, so let us experiment further. A careful study of the message gives us one very useful clue. The eighth word (ENCUU) ends in UU. There are no ordinary words ending in *aa* or *ii*. Only a very few words end in *nn* or *rr*. On the other hand, a fair number end in *ss*. So let us assume that U = *s*.

This offers another possible clue. There are two two-letter words in the message beginning with K (KU and KP). If U = *s*, then KU must be either *as*, *is*, or *us*, for there are no other two-letter words ending in *s*. K must therefore stand for *a*, *i*, or *u*. But which of these?

The other two-letter word (KP) will help us here. If KU = *us*, KP would have to stand for some other two-letter word beginning with *u*. The only possible word is *up*, and P = *p* is not likely in a substitution cipher, so let us examine other possibilities first.

If K does not stand for *u*, it must stand for either *a* or *i*. We examine these two possibilities in turn.

There are four common two-letter words in English beginning with *a*—namely, *am*, *an*, *as*, and *at*. The last two can be discarded, for we have already assumed that U = *s* and that V = *t*. If K = *a*, then KP must stand for either *am* or *an*.

The best way to check these possibilities is to look at the words before and after KP. The word which follows is VJG (= *the*), and *an the* does not make sense. Next, the only word in the language which can precede *am* is the pronoun *I*, but the word which precedes KP is a three-letter word (DQA). So it seems pretty certain that KP does not stand for either *an* or *am*, and therefore that K cannot stand for *a*.

Now let us experiment with K = *i*. There are five common two-letter words beginning with *i*—namely, *if, I'm, in, is*, and *it*. The last two, as before, can be discarded. We try the remaining three with the words which precede and follow. All three could quite well be preceded by a three-letter word, and *if the, I'm the*, and *in the* all make sense. We must therefore look a little more closely.

We find that the cipher letter P occurs also as the next-to-last letter in the tenth word (VTAKPI). Which of our three letters (*f, m, n*) is the most likely to occur in such a position? The letter *n* is frequently to be found as the next-to-last letter of a six-letter word (*nd* and *ng* are very common endings). Moreover, *n* is the only one of the three letters to be in the list of the nine commonest letters.

We will therefore assume to start with that K = *i* and that P = *n*.

Now we have:

```
-ete- is the--e-e-est -o- in the ---ss -t
RGVGT KU VJG ENGXGTGUV DQA KP VJG ENCUU CV
t--in-to so--e -i-he-s
VTAKPI VQ UQNXG EKRJGTU
```

A significant point strikes us at once. The ninth word is CV (= -*t*). It cannot be *it* for we already have K = *i*. It must therefore be *at*. In that case C = *a*, and the preceding word must end in *ass*. This suggests *class, brass, glass*, or *grass*. We take these in order. If ENCUU =

class, then E = *c* and N = *l.* This would make the fourth word *cle-e-est* and the last word *ci-he-s.*

There is nothing to suggest that these are unlikely. On the contrary, the words *cleverest* and *ciphers* immediately suggest themselves, and T = *r* fits both words. Moreover, R = *p* gives us *Peter* as the first word of the message, and X = *v* gives us *solve* as the next-to-last word.

We now have:

Peter is the cleverest -o- in the class at tr-in- to solve ciphers

No one should have much trouble in finishing this!

For a Substitution cipher involving figures or other symbols, precisely the same kind of approach is made. For example, if a count of figures in a numerical cipher gave us, say, 22 (9), 15 (8), 4 (7), we would begin by assuming that 22 = *e.* If this looked promising we would then try to see if 15 stood for *t* (or *n, o, a, i*), and whether 4 stood for one of these or for one of the other common letters (*r, s, h*).

Here are three more fairly straightforward cipher messages to break. Begin by making a letter or number count.

(i) LSP MPDL HEJ LZ LCJ EYO MCPEV E DPNCPL
XPDDERP TD LZ PIAPCTXPYL EYO APCDPGPCP

(ii) 15,25,19 17,5,2,2 21,9,9 20,6,9 20,22,9,13,21,19,22,9
12,9,6,5,26,10 13 21,9,11,22,9,20 24,13,26,9,2
12,9,26,9,13,20,6 20,6,9 3,5,20,11,6,9,26 21,5,26,3

(iii) 9,8,34,33,8 6,35,8 32,34,32,8,14,10 36,2 9,34,10,6
10,8,34,6 31,2 14,36,10,8 1,34,14,12,8,2 34,6 8,2,12
36,4 34,33,8,2,3,8

AIDS TO CODE-BREAKING

The example of code-breaking given in the last chapter is a fairly simple one, intended merely to show one way in which the problem may be approached. Things do not always run as smoothly as this. Where the words of the message are disguised by the use of, say, five-letter words, or by running all the letters or symbols together, solving the cipher will become a much more difficult task.

It would be too lengthy a business to go through the complicated processes by which an expert cryptanalyst attempts to break a subtle cipher. But here are some of the technical points which he constantly bears in mind.

One-letter words: a, I
Common two-letter words: of, to, in, it, is, at, be, we, on, he, if, go
Common three-letter words: the, and, for, are, but, you, not, can, was, has, had
Common four-letter words: that, with, from, this, will, have, were, your, they, when, here, more
Common double letters: ss, ee, tt, ff, ll, mm, oo
Common first letters: t, o, a, w, b, c, d, s, r
Common last letters: e, s, t, d, n, r, y
Common digraphs: th, er, on, an, re, he, in, ed, nd, ou, le, es. (A digraph is two letters occurring together anywhere in a word—e.g., THey, alTHough, wiTH.)
Common trigraphs: the, ent, ion, ing, tio, nce, tha, nde
Word Patterns: Many words have one or more letters repeated. If you number these letters, you find that the numbers present a kind of pattern. Such patterns can

be helpful in enabling a cryptanalyst to recognize a word. Here are some patterns of commonly used words:

- - 11 - 11	- 1 - - 11 -		- 1 - 1 - - 1			
poSSeSS	bEtwEEn		rEcEivE			
- 1 1 2 1 2	- 11 - - 22	12 - - 12 - -		1 2 2 - 1	- 1 2 2 - - 1	
nEEDED	aDDreSS	POstPOne		SEEmS	mESSagE	
1 2 2 1 - - -	- 1 2 2 1 - -		- 1 2 2 1 - -	- 1 2 2 1 - -	1 2 2 1	
ARRAnge	wILLIng		mISSIng	mISSIon	NOON	
- 1 2 2 1 -	- 1 2 2 1 -		- 1 2 2 1 -	1 - 22 - 11		
cOMMOn	bOTTOm		fOLLOw	SuCCeSS		
1 2 3 1 - 2 3	- - 1 2 3 1 2 3		1 - 2 3 2 1 3	1 2 3 2 3 - 2 1		
PREPaRE	brINGING		OpINION	REMEMbER		

Make a further list of your own on similar lines.

When you are trying to solve a Substitution cipher, try numbering letters that seem to be repeated, and then see if they conform to any of the word patterns in your lists.

PRACTICE ACTIVITIES

Activity No. 1
The following is a general knowledge quiz. The questions are set in the type of cipher indicated after each question. Answers should be given in the same cipher. The number of words required in the answer is shown in square brackets.

1. XIP XSPUF UIF OPWFM *EBWJE DPQQFS-GJFME?* (The one-ahead system, page 1.) [2]

2. ZKDW LV WKH KLJKHVW PRXQWDLQ LQ WKH ZRUOG? (Julius Caesar cipher, page 2.) [2]

3. CWPHR AMTSC OOBNL TURVO DLWSR TVHYE STRIN DOEPS? (The five-letter-word system, page 7.) [2]

4. PU DOHA WSHFH KVLZ ZOFSVJR HWWLHY? (The key letter system, page 4.) [4]

5. ebbcaadd bddc ddbcae acaacebdddaaca cdba dbdedcdcbdaa? (Bishop Wilkins's system, page 9.) [1]

6. 4, 19, 26, 7, 23, 12, 7, 19, 22, 18, 13, 18, 7, 18, 26, 15, 8, 25, 25, 24, 8, 7, 26, 13, 23, 21, 12, 9? (The number system, with 1 = Z, page 16.) [3]

7. DEA ECB DAA ECB DBE CCA ECC CCC BDA BCB CAA EBA DAD ACB CAD AAE ABE CAA? (Bishop Wilkins's system adapted, page 11.) [2]

8. EWOTH VANDT RIDES ATOSH BEORF DINER ISNOT OBLOO POSHK SORUF ITBAH FERLB RISLB FLAME? (The five-letter-word system, page 7.) [1]

9. 12, 24, 18, 12, 13, 3, 7, 8, 19, 3, 11, 2, 19, 17, 3, 8, 14, 23, 9, 26, 18, 7, 18, 20, 19, 6, 18, 20, 9, 26, 19, 5? (The number cipher, three-column system, page 17.) [2]

10. ALEX MW XLI REQI SJ LMW LSQI? (The four-ahead system, page 4.) [2]

Activity No. 2

For instructions, see Practice Activity 1.

1. XIBU TFUV WG QOAZ SBE AMVLQVO XIPIKVETL NFTTBHFT? (The "Brownie" system, page 5.) [2: Begin your answer at the B of "Brownie."]

2. ∧⊐⊓ ∧⌐∨ ⊏⌐⊓⊓∧⌐ ⌐∨ ∨⊐∟ ⊏⌐∪> ∧⊔∨⊐ ⌐ ⊏⌐⊓⊓? (The Ticktacktoe system, regular order, page 25.) [2]

3. 4328292 328404 3352 335323 538393 321312 5273825 2534? (The number cipher, without commas, page 19.) [3]

4.
K	W	T	H	E	O
W	N	R	A	A	R
A	C	I	M	E	L
S	H	I	N	D	E
T	S	I	C	M	P
L	H	I	E	T	O

(The Cardan grill. If you have not cut a grill, you can copy the above letters on a piece of transparent paper exactly the same size as the grill in the book, page 30. Put the paper over the grill, and note the letters which lie on the black squares.) [2: Put an X for each null in the answer.]

5. QOJ LSWYNL GA T CFX PQMSRFMNU? (The revolving circle, page 39.) [6: Begin your answer at A = X.]

6.

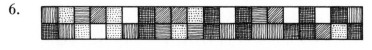

(Color cipher, page 36.) [2]

7. >⊐⌐⌐ ⊓∟ ∟⊐⊐ ⊐⊓∨⊐⊐∟∟ ⊓⌐⊓<
⊓□ ∟⊐⊐ ⊔□⊓∟⊐⌐ ∟∟⌐⊔∟⊐∟ ⌐⊓<⌐?

(The Ticktacktoe system, irregular order, page 27.) [3]

8. UYHO ECHW EFNK GEHO SRAI NMIA NNAI RSOY VMAG LWEE CLEL OBHI ENNT TDAY? (The Crossword grill, page 33.) [3]

9. DEAEC BDECE CBDBA BDBAE ABBDB
AADAE DBCBC CABCE ECDBA EABAD CBCAA
ACBBD BAABC EDAEA?
(Bishop Wilkins's system adapted, page 10.) [3]

10. ⦾⦾⦾⦾⦾○⦾⦾⦾○⦾⦾⦾⦾⦾⦾⦾⦾⦾⦾○⦾⦾⦾⦾⦾○
⦾⦾⦾⦾⦾⦾⦾⦾⦾⦾⦾⦾⦾⦾⦾⦾○⦾⦾⦾○⦾⦾⦾⦾⦾⦾⦾⦾⦾

(Color cipher in dots, page 36.) [3: Give your answer
in colored dots large enough to be clear.]

Activity No. 3
These questions are all set in ciphers explained in this
book, but you are left to find out for yourself which
ciphers they are. Give your answer in the same cipher as
the question.

1. RWCHB OXWMA USLTY HYEPF BRIES
NWCAH YGPEA NVEZR KAILM WFHRO
EFKOY UAGSH PTBIR NOTCH XECAD
MUEBR MIYCZ AINSR TETVL OTLBU DTVIU
OMNBP? [4]

2. VXKT CPBT DUP UXGHI EGTHXSTCI DU
IWT JCXITS HIPITH. [2]

3. 12, 24, 13, 11, 8, 3, 26, 24, 23, 1, 18, 3, 11, 7, 13, 1, 18,
20, 3, 4, 18, 25, 6, 13, 9, 18, 8, 9, 3, 8, 6, 8, 25, 5? [2]

4. DFEB PFW AZJD CF SIF MZPKLQMQ ZRP
HAUVX VHFGAHI ZKR ZUBTC XVQA. [2]

5. DEAEB AEEAE BADAD BAEAB AEBAA

DAEAB DADBB ECBDC CADBE CBACA BACAE
CBEAB CEBAE EECEA? [2]

6. HATM ANTL LEWE EAER EZAC LADI LMSS
IEAE AONN LNPF SCBI TWCD ARDI OASC. [8]

7. TUBUF KYV BOAS KB GUR NQZAB QER UP
JVK ID W CEVAGVAT XZMAA MR ZLDQHBZ.
[2]

8. 293 4432829 232839282 13125 393625 21382 521
343632 2145 43213 921232 821382 12340 2538 272
9422 534 213 42 1393 9 39282 52124? [4]

9.

A	E	M	X	S	P
L	T	E	R	A	T
T	A	S	H	E	A
I	N	D	N	L	F
E	M	W	H	O	A
N	T	D	T	P	R

[4]

10. CNGZ IURUXY XKYVKIZOBKRE GXK ZNK
IXUYY GTJ HGIQMXUATJ UL ZNK YCOYY
LRGM? [2]

Activity No. 4

Each enciphered question is written in a way slightly
different from the examples given in the appropriate
chapter of the book. Can you discover the differences
and read the questions? Answer in the same cipher with
the same difference.

1. DEAEB AEEAE CDDAE ECBDB DACDB EECCA
BACAC DDDAB CADBA BCDAA DBAEA BDBCD
ABBDA BCCAE CDCBC AABCD?
(Fairly straightforward, but some extras have
slipped in.) [3]

2. CEHXANP OBR DFWWTGLY BWTYJ CP
IJYLU TFU EJ XODOB: RTGP NYX PCOG
(The "Brownie" system, but using a different key
word or key words. There is a connection with
"Brownie.") [2]

3. 20, 11, 13, 11, 6   9, 13, 18, 6   1, 24   11, 7, 17
24, 13, 18, 1, 3, 20   13, 9, 23, 25, 6, 9, 26
20, 11, 1, 9, 6   23, 25, 2, 23, 8, 17   9, 17, 13, 2
20, 13, 8, 25, 20, 5, 3, 2, 22   6, 9, 15, 8, 13, 9, 14
(It's the three-column system, page 17, but there's a
switch of columns.) [1]

4. (cipher symbols)

(Work it out as in the *Adjust* diagram, page 26, and
see what you get.) [3: He discovered ———]

5. OKL VGTQ HQ CWFWCM FXSJG LEVX
RFPQZX? [4: The discovery ——— ———.]
(Don't start with A = X this time.)

6. RBNFA TUMLE SCTFH VDEKF UNIER JCSYT
BXMHA FTNGI BLNWS YTPEA LDCJE
(Not the revolving circle, at any rate.) [2]

7.
W	L	A	I	I	G
H	H	E	F	T	R
O	P	I	M	A	R
S	L	A	X	D	N
E	S	Y	Z	E	T
T	T	W	H	O	F

(The Cardan grill, but it starts in a different way.)
[7: W— and O— — did at K—. (No nulls are needed.)]

8. HZFWO JZF PIAPNE EZ QTYO APYRFTYD LE ESP YZCES AZWP ZC LE ESP DZFES AZWP?
(Try your hand at code-breaking.)   [3]

9. 44314 33550 3835 43454 451433 54450 49503 1443 4394 4373 1505038 353 5445048 31443 33550 45443 55355 45484 138314 83245 48
(Start a bit higher than 21 and include the whole alphabet.)   [4]

10. LAMO OANN LWTS AEHI HWUC EEER ATYO NFYY KRTO OWBE EGLT XBJI HLHE AVAE?
(Try working upward. Give first name and surname in each case.)   [8]

Activity No. 5
A Classroom Treasure Hunt
For this activity the class should be divided into teams consisting of, say, four or five members each. The

number of teams will depend on the size of the class, but there should be an even number. Each team is allotted a section of the classroom, or any wider area of the school, at the teacher's discretion. Each team leader is also given a card labeled TREASURE.

Six clues are written (see below), each in a different cipher. All these clues, and the TREASURE card, must be hidden in different places within the team's allotted area. Each clue will lead to the hiding place of the next clue; the last clue, of course, will lead to where the TREASURE card is hidden.

Teams should be arranged in pairs, each team competing against the team with which it has been paired. The winning team is the first to find a TREASURE card.

The project should preferably be arranged to take place in about five stages.

Stage 1. The selection and pairing of teams. The name of each team may be written on a slip, and the slips drawn in pairs from a hat.

Stage 2. The decision as to where the clues are to be hidden. Each team must, of course, arrange this privately by whatever arrangement the teacher prefers. Clues to hiding places might be on the following lines: "Look for the next clue inside the copy of *Black Beauty* in Mary's desk" or "The third clue is hidden underneath the chalk box in the corner cupboard."

Stage 3. The writing of the clues. They should be written in the order shown below. Each clue should consist of not less than *ten* words and not more than *twenty* words.

Clue 1: The Julius Caesar cipher (page 2).
Clue 2: The color cipher, squares or dots (page 36).
Clue 3: The three-column number cipher (page 17).
Clue 4: The scytale (page 13). The size of the scytale

may be agreed upon beforehand by both teams, or (if the teams are sufficiently advanced) they may be left to discover for themselves, by experiment, what size has been used.

Clue 5: The pencil-dot or pinprick cipher (page 21). The chosen passage should consist of not less than twenty lines and not more than sixty lines. The passage may either be cut out or left for the team to find in the newspaper, but the arrangement should be the same for *all* teams.

Clue 6: The Cardan grill (page 30).

IMPORTANT. The clues must be *accurately written* in the appropriate cipher. Each clue should be checked by more than one member of the team. Any team offering an incorrectly written clue should be disqualified from winning.

Stage 4. The hiding of the clues. Each team should, of course, be given a chance to hide its clues privately.

Stage 5. The working out of the clues. The first clue will be handed to each team leader at the same time.

NOTE. Other ciphers may be substituted for or added to those given in Stage 3, at the teacher's discretion. For the more advanced pupils further projects of this kind may be arranged, with clues similar to those in Practice Activities 3 and 4.